The Cato Institute

The Cato Institute is named for the libertarian pamphlets, *Cato's Letters*, which were inspired by the Roman Stoic, Cato the Younger. Written by John Trenchard and Thomas Gordon, *Cato's Letters* were widely read in the American colonies in the early eighteenth century and played a major role in laying the philosophical foundation for the revolution that followed.

The erosion of civil and economic liberties in the modern world has occurred in concert with a widening array of social problems. These disturbing developments have resulted from a major failure to examine social problems in terms of the fundamental principles of human dignity, economic welfare, and justice.

The Cato Institute aims to broaden public policy debate by sponsoring programs designed to assist both the scholar and the concerned layperson in analyzing questions of political economy.

The programs of the Cato Institute include the sponsorship and publication of basic research in social philosophy and public policy; publication of major journals on the scholarship of liberty and commentary on political affairs; production of debate forums for radio; and organization of an extensive program of symposia, seminars, and conferences.

CATO INSTITUTE
1700 Montgomery Street
San Francisco, California 94111

Unemployment and Monetary Policy

Unemployment and Monetary Policy

Government as Generator of the "Business Cycle"

by Friedrich A. Hayek

With a Foreword by Gerald P. O'Driscoll, Jr.

CATO PAPER No. 3

CATO INSTITUTE
San Francisco, California

Publisher's Note: This *Cato Paper* was originally published in
July 1975 by The Institute of Economic Affairs, London, as
Occasional Paper No. 45. The present edition has been revised
for the American reader.

Printed in the United States of America.

CATO INSTITUTE
1700 Montgomery Street
San Francisco, California 94111

CONTENTS

Foreword   *Gerald P. O'Driscoll, Jr.*   ix

A Note on Austrian
Capital Theory   *Sudha R. Shenoy*   xv

Preface   xvii

Part I. Inflation, Misdirection of Labor,
and Unemployment   1

   1. Inflation and Unemployment   3

      Three choices in policy   Lessons of the Great Inflation

   2. Keynes's Political "Cure"
      for Unemployment   6

      Development of Keynesian ideas   The "fatal idea"

   3. The True Theory of Unemployment   8

      Keynes's theory — a temptation to politicians
      Floating exchanges, full employment,
      and stable currency

   4. Inflation Ultimately
      Increases Unemployment   11

      Why we cannot live with inflation
      Harmful effects of inflation   The misdirection
      of labor   The consequences are unavoidable
      Temporary, not mass, unemployment

   5. What Can Be Done Now?   15

      The first step   Prevent recession from
      degenerating into depression   The Keynesian dream
      Primary aim: stable money, not unstable "full
      employment"   Disciplining the monetary authorities

Part II. The Pretense of Knowledge   21

The "scientistic" attitude   The chief cause of
unemployment   Mathematical method in economics:
uses and limitations   When science is unscientific
Obstacles to prediction   Power to coerce may
impede spontaneous forces

Part III. Unemployment: Inevitable
Consequence of Inflation   37

Keynes confirmed business's belief in high
demand   "Secondary depression" and monetary
countermeasures   Difficult to discover the
misdirected labor in the "long prosperity"
Recovery must come from a revival of profitable
investment   Monetarism and the mechanical
(macro) quantity theory   Cantillon and Keynes
Governments have acted on poor advice
"Inflation": true and false   No choice between
inflation and unemployment

Recommended Reading   47

About the Author   53

FOREWORD

The fallacy of the nonexhaustive choice

It is now widely recognized that the concepts and methodology of traditional macroeconomics can be related only with the greatest difficulty (if at all) to general economic theory. Macroeconomics deals with such aggregate concepts as national income, aggregate demand, total employment, velocity, etc. Until comparatively recently, macrotheorists have not focused on the microfoundations for macrotheory. Instead, a good deal of professional effort has been devoted to the "Fiscalist vs. Monetarist" or "Keynesian vs. Friedmanite" debates.

That these debates directed attention away from the microfoundations problem is only part of the problem. These debates were largely futile. The issues separating the protagonists were generally neither what they perceived them to be at the time,[1] nor what textbook writers portrayed them to be. Further, the juxtaposition of the two alternatives—the neoquantity theory vs. Keynesianism—involves the fallacy of the nonexhaustive choice. Standard monetarist and Keynesian models represent a very small range in the spectrum of approaches to the problem of economic fluctuations. The views of Professor Hayek and other proponents of the "Austrian" theory of fluctuations always represented a genuine alternative to macro orthodoxy. That their views were almost never mentioned in macroeconomic discussions surely reflects, at least in part, the fact that to have included them would have meant both redefining the contours of the debate and recognizing the sterility of earlier discussion.

The macro orthodoxy is, of course, now shattered. It is trite but

---

[1] For an illustration of the difficulties economists have had in specifying what the issues were, see the symposium on Milton Friedman's monetary theory in the *Journal of Political Economy* 80 (September/October 1972).

accurate to observe that Keynesianism as we knew it is dead intellectually, however long its ideas may survive in textbooks and books by popular writers. It is true that there are a great number of "neo-Keynesian" (or "post-Keynesian") models. In this context, I agree with Professor Yeager's cogent argument that recent "Keynesian" theorists show undue modesty in ascribing their original contributions to Keynes.[2]

Likewise, for better or for worse, monetarism is being supplanted by the new Rational Expectations theory, about which more will be said shortly.

Hayek rediscovered

The renewed interest in Hayek's views reflects a search for alternative formulations. Hayek, Keynes's early and most effective intellectual opponent, dissented from Keynes's formulation of the problem of economic fluctuations in terms of aggregative concepts of the emergent macrotheory. Hayek argued vigorously that these concepts were mere mental constructs, not meaningful empirical categories. He pointed out that general economic theory forcefully demonstrated the impossibility of stable functional relationships among such macro variables as consumption and investment, or total employment and investment. Not only the magnitude of the coefficients but also their algebraic signs must change over the course of a business cycle.

Hayek's critique of Keynes's system paralleled his earlier critique of the quantity theory for lacking micro foundations.[3] Indeed, by implication Hayek identified the strong connection between the quantity theory and its supposed opposite, Keynesianism. If one were to pursue this connection, one would go a long way toward explaining the futility of macro debates.[4]

---

[2]Leland Yeager, "The Keynesian Diversion," *Western Economic Journal* 11 (June 1973):150-63.

[3]See Friedrich A. Hayek, *Prices and Production,* 2d ed. (London: Routledge & Kegan Paul, 1935), pp. 1-31 and *passim.*

[4]For a preliminary attempt to do this, see Gerald P. O'Driscoll, Jr., and Sudha R. Shenoy, "Inflation, Recession, and Stagflation," in *The Foundations of Modern Austrian Economics,* ed. Edwin G. Dolan (Kansas City: Sheed & Ward, 1976), pp. 185-211.

This interpretation also explains why Hayek's approach was not integrated into textbook discussions. In *Monetary Theory and the Trade Cycle,* Hayek called for an integration of monetary and price theory.[5] In *Prices and Production,* drawing on the monetary theory of his teacher Ludwig von Mises, he outlined a theory in which monetary disturbances alter the array of relative prices by affecting market interest rates and the pattern of investment. Monetary injections constitute an additional source of demand for goods and resources; the market signals (i.e., prices) generated by this additional source will be reacted to as though real factors (e.g., savings preferences) had changed. Transactors respond to market signals, and the relevant signals indicate that the underlying functions have changed.

Indeed, for a time, the effects of monetary expansion could be the same as that generated by a shift of savings preferences in favor of future as opposed to current consumption. An "investment boom" and high employment would result. Crucial to Hayek's analysis is the observation that resources will be attracted into productive activities that would not otherwise have existed. The resources can remain so employed only as long as the monetary expansion continues. The rate of increase in the money stock must accelerate to maintain the (disequilibrium) pattern of employment.

It is not true that high employment either depends upon or can be sustained permanently by monetary expansion; the contrary is an implication of Hayek's analysis, as he explains in the first essay. But once monetary expansion has produced real effects, the resulting pattern of resource allocation can only be maintained, if at all, by accelerations in the rate of growth of the money stock. As Hayek notes in the first essay, unemployment is not a means of combating inflation (as Keynesian macrotheory erroneously suggests), but the result of slowing the rate of growth of the money stock. Once the money-augmented demand for resources is reduced in the sectors in which it previously expanded, entrepreneurs will begin reallocating resources, including labor services.

[5]Friedrich A. Hayek, *Monetary Theory and the Trade Cycle* (1933), trans. N. Kaldor and H. M. Croome (New York: Kelley, 1966).

What is perceived as a problem of *aggregate* unemployment by those who impose mental constructs of macroeconomics upon the world, is in reality a *sectoral* unemployment problem. In turn, sectoral unemployment in one period is, in this instance, the result of overemployment in these sectors in previous periods. (Symmetrically, there has been underemployment of resources elsewhere.)

It is important to note that it is in expansions, *generated by money creation* (as opposed to genuine saving), that misallocations and entrepreneurial errors occur. What is termed a "recession" merely reveals previous allocational errors, and it is in the recessionary phase that corrective reallocations occur. This insight explains why recessions are necessary to restore equilibrium; the recession *is* (the beginning of) the restoration of equilibrium. For policy-makers to commit themselves to ending inflation without a recession of some kind is to commit themselves to the impossible; but this commitment ensures continued and accelerating inflation, along with economic stagnation. There are no "soft landings" for an economy in which the coordination of economic activities has been disrupted by inflation.

Though Hayek's first and third essays build on his early theoretical work, they are applications for the seventies and eighties, with particular reference to Britain. There is little in these essays, written in 1975, that is dated. References to labor union power as the ultimate reason for money creation will, however, strike many U.S. readers as odd. Whatever may be true of Britain, it is difficult to saddle U.S. labor unions with being the cause of monetary expansion in the United States. Regardless, however, of the source of pressures for monetary expansion, resource allocation is affected by monetary policy. Even if monetary expansion is no longer substantially directed to stimulating private investment, as Hayek suggested it was in 1931, economic coordination and the allocation of resources is interfered with.

Recent theoretical developments

The Rational Expectations theorists sounded the death knell of Keynesian macroeconomics. Indeed, in pointing out the reasons why macroeconometric models *must* fail in simulating the effects of alternative macro policies, Professor Robert Lucas and others were echoing points made by Hayek forty years ago.[6] In fact, in his Nobel Memorial Lecture (the second essay), Hayek restates his position forcefully and provides methodological foundations for his positive analysis.

While recognizing that in their critiques of conventional macroeconomics, Rational Expectations theorists repeat Hayekian insights, one must not overlook fundamental differences between Hayek and the new monetary theory. Hayek always emphasized that markets operate with an economy of information, and that they are characterized by decentralization and dispersion of knowledge.[7] This insight explains both the efficiency of markets *and* their vulnerability to monetary disturbances. The structure of the economy is revealed to no one. Expectations are formed because complete knowledge is lacking. In their emphasis on the homogeneity of knowledge sets and transactors' knowing the structure of the economy, Rational Expectations theorists diverge radically from Hayek's approach.[8]

One should surely be heartened by recent developments in monetary theory. But monetary theory has yet to rediscover the specific contributions of Mises, Hayek, and the other "Austrians" to our understanding of economic fluctuations. Theirs is a tradition, beginning with Cantillon and tracing through classical political economy, that has been ignored. This *Cato Paper* serves as an excellent introduction to that tradition.

February 1979

Gerald P. O'Driscoll, Jr.
New York University

[6]See Robert E. Lucas, Jr., "Econometric Policy Evaluation: A Critique," in *The Phillips Curve and Labor Markets,* ed. Karl Brunner and Allan H. Meltzer (New York: North-Holland, 1976), pp. 19-46.

[7]Friedrich A. Hayek, "Economics and Knowledge" and "The Use of Knowledge in Society," in his *Individualism and Economic Order* (Chicago: University of Chicago Press, 1948).

[8]In his recent criticism of the Rational Expectations approach, Professor Arrow adopts the Hayekian position. See Kenneth J. Arrow, "The Future and Present in Economics," *Economic Inquiry* 61 (April 1978): 157-71.

A NOTE ON
AUSTRIAN CAPITAL THEORY

Austrian capital theory views capital not as a homogeneous stock but as a network of interrelated goods: a diversified structure of complementary elements, rather than a uniform lump. The process of production is seen as occurring in a series of "stages," extending from final consumption to stages successively further removed. To take a simple example: A steel mill *by itself* cannot produce final consumption goods, like cars or washing machines. In order to produce such consumer goods, a whole intervening chain of complementary investments is required: in factories, machinery, stocks of raw materials, etc. The steel mill's output passes into the next stage of production as an input, together with other inputs (raw materials, etc.), and is used in the factories in this stage to produce various intermediate goods. These goods in turn serve as inputs for the next stage of production, until final consumption is reached.

Thus, investments in wholesale and retail distribution, in this view, are complementary to investments in previous stages of production; they are an integral part of the capital structure as a whole necessary to bring goods to the final consumption stage. Particular capital goods may be specific to one stage of production, or they may be adaptable to several stages.

In other words, a miscellaneous jumble of nonconsumption goods will *not necessarily* raise final output. Individual capital investments (whether in plant, machinery, raw materials or semifinished goods) must fit into an integrated capital structure, completed to the final consumption stage, if they are to add to final consumption output. Investments that do not form such an integrated structure are (or become) *mal*-investments yielding capital and operating losses.

The "filigree" (i.e., composition) of capital goods forming a coordinated capital structure changes with circumstances. Thus a factory, once profitable, becomes unprofitable as the circumstances in which it was originally built are themselves altered. Equally, new investment opportunities open up with changing circumstances; investments once useless may become profitable again. In short, capital is *not* automatically maintained intact; neither is any investment automatically profitable in all circumstances.

The essential role of prices (and of rates of return on individual goods) emerges from this brief outline. Only if there exist markets in which prices reflect (changing) relative scarcities of the different sorts of capital goods involved can the capital structure as a whole be integrated, and mal-investments be revealed.

Sudha R. Shenoy

PREFACE

The present unemployment is the direct result of the shortsighted "full employment policies" we have been pursuing for the past twenty-five years. This is the sad truth we must grasp if we are not to be led into measures that will only make matters worse. The sooner we can find our way out of the fool's paradise in which we have been living, the shorter will be the period of suffering.

Nothing is easier than creating additional employment for a time by drawing workers into activities made temporarily attractive by the expenditure of additional money created for that purpose. Indeed, during the past twenty-five years we have deliberately and systematically resorted to the quick provision of employment precisely by increasing the supply of money, which during the preceding 200 years had been regularly increasing as a result of a defect in the credit system—thus becoming the cause of recurrent depressions.

We should not be surprised at this result, inasmuch as we have successively removed all the barriers erected in the past as defenses against the ever-present popular pressure for "cheap money." What happened at the beginning of the period of modern finance has happened again—we have been seduced by another silver-tongued persuader into trying another inflationary bubble. And that bubble has now burst. We shall soon discover that much of the artificially induced "growth" was a waste of resources and that the harsh truth is that the West is living beyond its means.

Urgent as is the need to reintegrate the jobless into the productive process, if we are to prevent similar calamities in the future, it is no less important that we avoid making matters worse by repeating the mistakes made in the recent past. It is to this most urgent task of rethinking the theoretical conceptions that have guided us that the lectures here printed are addressed.

The first two lectures were delivered to academic audiences in Italy[1] and Sweden,[2] and were destined for publication in the memoirs of the learned institutions to which they were presented. The third, added when the first two were already set in type, contains elaborations and elucidations I found necessary to add when I pursued the themes of the first during a lecture trip in the United States.[3]

I am very grateful to the Cato Institute for making these lectures available to readers in the United States by including them in the Institute's series of *Cato Papers.*

March 1979   F. A. Hayek

---

[1] "Inflation, Misdirection of Labor, and Unemployment" is a revised version of a lecture delivered on February 8, 1975, to the "Convegno Internazionale: Il Problema della Moneta Oggi," organized in commemoration of the 100th birthday of Luigi Einaudi by the Academia Nazionale dei Lincei at Rome and published in the proceedings of that congress.

[2] "The Pretense of Knowledge," an Alfred Nobel Memorial Lecture, was delivered on December 11, 1974, at the Stockholm School of Economics.

[3] "Unemployment: Inevitable Consequence of Inflation." Lecture delivered at various places in the United States during April 1975.

PART I.
Inflation, Misdirection of Labor, and Unemployment

1. Inflation and Unemployment

After a unique quarter-century of great prosperity, the economy of the Western world has arrived at a critical point. I expect that the period will enter history under the name of the Great Prosperity, just as the 1930s are known as the Great Depression.

By eliminating the automatic brakes that operated in the past (namely, the gold standard and fixed rates of exchange), we have indeed succeeded in maintaining the full employment—and even overemployment—created by an expansion of credit and ultimately prolonged by open inflation. We have, in fact, succeeded in maintaining this for a much longer time than I should have thought possible. But the inevitable end is now near, or perhaps it has already arrived.

I find myself in an unpleasant situation. I had preached for forty years that the time to prevent the coming of a depression is during the boom. During the boom nobody listened to me. Now people again turn to me and ask how we can avoid the consequences of a policy about which I had constantly warned. I must witness the heads of the governments of all the Western industrial countries promising their people that they will stop the inflation *and* preserve full employment. But I know that they *cannot* do this. I even fear that attempts to postpone the inevitable crisis by a new inflationary push may temporarily succeed and make the eventual breakdown even worse.

Three choices in policy

The disquieting but unalterable truth is that a false monetary and credit policy, pursued through almost the entire post-World War

II period, has placed the economic systems of all the Western industrial countries in a highly unstable position—one in which *anything* we do will produce most unpleasant consequences. We have only three choices:

1. To allow a rapidly accelerating open inflation to continue until it has brought about a complete disorganization of all economic activity.

2. To impose controls of wages and prices that would for a time conceal the effects of a continued inflation but would inevitably lead to a centrally directed, totalitarian economic system.

3. To terminate resolutely the increase in the quantity of money—a step that would soon, through the appearance of substantial unemployment, make manifest all the misdirections of labor that the inflation of the past years has caused and that the other two procedures would further increase.

Lessons of the Great Inflation

To understand why the whole Western world allowed itself to be led into this frightful dilemma, it is necessary to glance back briefly at two events that occurred soon after World War I and that largely determined the views governing the policy of the post-World War II years. First I want to recall an experience that has unfortunately been largely forgotten. In Austria and Germany the Great Inflation had directed our attention to the connection between changes in the quantity of money and changes in the degree of employment. It especially showed us that the employment created by inflation diminished as soon as the inflation slowed down, and that the termination of the inflation always produced what came to be called a "stabilization crisis," with substantial unemployment. It was the insight into this connection that made me and some of my contemporaries reject and oppose from the outset the kind of full employment policy propagated by Lord Keynes and his followers.

To this recollection of the Great Inflation I must add an acknowledgment of how much I learned, not only from personal observation, but also from being taught to see—mostly by my teacher, the late Ludwig von Mises—the utter stupidity of the

4

arguments then propounded, especially in Germany, to explain and justify the increases in the quantity of money. Most of these arguments I am now encountering again in the countries, not the least Great Britain and the United States, that then seemed better trained in economics and whose economists rather looked down at the foolishness of their German colleagues. None of these apologists for the inflationary policy was able to propose or apply measures to terminate the inflation, which was finally ended by Hjalmar Schacht, a man who firmly believed in a crude and primitive version of the quantity theory.

The policy of the recent decades, or the theory that underlies it, had its origin, however, in the specific experiences of Great Britain during the 1920s and 1930s. After what now seems the very modest inflation of the First World War, Great Britain returned to the gold standard in 1925; in my opinion very sensibly and honestly, but unfortunately and unwisely at the former parity. This had in no way been required by classical doctrine: David Ricardo wrote to a friend in 1821, "I never should advise a government to restore a currency, which was depreciated 30 per cent, to par."[1] I often ask myself how different the economic history of the world might have been if, in the discussion during the years preceding 1925, just one English economist had remembered and pointed out this passage from Ricardo.

In any event, the unfortunate decision taken in 1925 made a prolonged process of deflation inevitable. This process might have been successful in maintaining the gold standard if it had been continued until a large part of the wages had been reduced. I believe this attempt was near success when, in the world crisis of 1931, Britain abandoned it along with the gold standard, which was thereby greatly discredited.

[1]Ricardo to Wheatley, 18 September 1821, reprinted in *The Works of David Ricardo,* ed. Piero Sraffa, vol. 9 (Cambridge: At the University Press, 1952), p. 73.

2. Keynes's Political "Cure" for Unemployment

Development of Keynesian ideas

It was during the period of extensive unemployment in Great Britain preceding the worldwide economic crisis of 1929-1931 that John Maynard Keynes developed his basic ideas. It is important to note that this development of his economic thought took place while his country was in a very exceptional and almost unique position: As a result of the big appreciation in the international value of the pound sterling, the real wages of practically all British workers had increased substantially compared with real wages in the rest of the world, and Britain had in consequence become unable to compete successfully with other countries. In order to give employment to the unemployed, it would have been necessary either to reduce practically *all* wages or to raise the sterling prices of most commodities.

It is possible to distinguish three distinct phases in the development of Keynes's thought. First, he began with the recognition that it was necessary to reduce real wages. Second, he arrived at the conclusion that this was *politically* impossible. Third, he convinced himself that it would be useless and even harmful. The Keynes of 1919 still understood that

> there is no subtler, no surer means of overturning the existing basis of society than to debauch the currency. The process engages all the hidden forces of economic law on the side of destruction, and does it in a manner which not one man in a million is able to diagnose.[2]

---

[2] "The Economic Consequences of the Peace," in *The Collected Writings of John Maynard Keynes,* vol. 2 (London: Macmillan for the Royal Economic Society, 1971), p. 149.

His political judgment made him the inflationist, or at least avid antideflationist, of the 1930s. I have, however, good reason to believe that he would have disapproved of what his followers did in the postwar period. If he had not died so soon, he would have become one of the leaders in the fight against inflation.

The "fatal idea"

It was in that unfortunate episode of English monetary history in which he became the intellectual leader that Keynes gained acceptance for the fatal idea, namely, that unemployment is predominantly due to an insufficiency of aggregate demand when compared with the total of wages that would have to be paid if all workers were employed at current rates.

This formula of employment as a direct function of total demand proved so extraordinarily effective because it seemed to be confirmed in some degree by the results of quantitative empirical data. In contrast, the alternative explanations of unemployment, which I regard as correct, could make no such claims. The dangerous effects that the "scientistic" prejudice has had in this diagnosis is the subject of my Nobel lecture at Stockholm (Part II). Briefly, we find the curious situation that the Keynesian theory, which is confirmed by statistics because it happens to be the only one that can be tested quantitatively, is nevertheless false. Yet it is widely accepted only because the explanation earlier regarded as true, and which I still regard as true, cannot *by its very nature* be tested by statistics.

3. The True Theory of Unemployment

The true, though untestable, explanation for extensive unemployment ascribes it to a discrepancy between the distribution of labor (and the other factors of production) among industries (and localities) and the distribution of demand among their products. This discrepancy is caused by a distortion of the system of *relative* prices and wages. And it can be corrected only by a change in these relations, that is, by establishing in each sector of the economy those prices and wages at which supply will equal demand.

The cause of unemployment, in other words, is a deviation from the equilibrium prices and wages that would establish themselves given a free market and stable money. But we can never know beforehand at what structure of relative prices and wages such an equilibrium would establish itself. We are therefore unable to measure the deviation of current prices from the equilibrium prices which makes it impossible to sell part of the labor supply. We are therefore also unable to demonstrate a statistical correlation between the distortion of relative prices and the volume of unemployment. Yet, although not measurable, causes may be very effective. The current superstition that only the measurable can be important has done much to mislead economists and the world in general.

Keynes's theory—a temptation to politicians

The fact that Keynesian theory provided the politicians with tempting opportunities was probably even more important than the fashionable prejudices concerning scientific method that made it attractive to professional economists. It offered not only a cheap and quick method of removing a major source of real

8

human suffering, but also a release from the most confining restrictions that had impeded their striving for popularity. Spending money and having budget deficits were suddenly represented as virtues. It was even argued persuasively that increased government expenditure was wholly meritorious, since it led to the utilization of hitherto unused resources, thus costing the community nothing and bringing it a net gain.

These beliefs led in particular to the gradual removal of all effective barriers to an increase in the quantity of money by the monetary authorities. The Bretton Woods agreement had tried to place the burden of international adjustment exclusively on the surplus countries, that is, to require them to expand but not to require the deficit countries to contract. It thus laid the foundation for a world inflation. But this was at least done in the laudable endeavor to secure fixed rates of exchange. Yet when the criticism of the inflation-minded majority of economists succeeded in removing this last obstacle to national inflation, no effective brake remained, as the experience of Britain since the late 1960s illustrates.

Floating exchanges, full employment, and stable currency

It is, I believe, undeniable that the demand for flexible rates of exchange originated wholly from countries such as Great Britain, some of whose economists wanted a wider margin for inflationary expansion (called "full employment policy"). They later received support, unfortunately, from other economists who were not inspired by the desire for inflation, but who seem to have overlooked the strongest argument in favor of fixed rates of exchange, namely, that they constitute the practically irreplaceable curb we need to *compel* the politicians, and the monetary authorities responsible to them, to maintain a stable currency.

The maintenance of the value of money and the avoidance of inflation constantly demand from the politicians highly unpopular measures. Only by showing that government is compelled to take these measures can the politicians justify them to people adversely affected. So long as the preservation of the external value of the national currency is regarded as an indisputable

9

necessity, as it is with fixed exchange rates, politicians can resist the constant demands for cheaper credits, for avoidance of a rise in interest rates, for more expenditure on "public works," and so on. With fixed exchanges, a fall in the foreign value of the currency, or an outflow of gold or foreign exchange reserves, acts as a signal requiring prompt government action. With flexible exchange rates, the effect of an increase in the quantity of money on the internal price level is much too slow to be generally apparent or to be charged to those ultimately responsible for it. Moreover, the inflation of prices is usually preceded by a welcome increase in employment; it may therefore even be welcomed because its harmful effects are not visible until later.

It is therefore easy to understand why, in the hope of restraining countries all too inclined toward inflation, other nations like Germany, itself noticeably suffering from imported inflation, hesitated in the postwar period to destroy altogether the system of fixed rates of exchange. For a time that seemed likely to restrain the temptation to further speed up inflation. But now that the system of fixed rates of exchange appears to have totally collapsed and scarcely any hope remains that self-discipline might induce some countries to restrain themselves, there is little reason to adhere to a system that is no longer effective. In retrospect one may even ask whether, out of a mistaken hope, the German Bundesbank or the Swiss National Bank waited too long, and then raised the value of their currency too little. But in the long run I do not believe we shall regain a system of international stability without returning to a system of fixed exchange rates, which imposes upon the national central banks the restraint essential for successfully resisting the pressure of the advocates of inflation in their countries—usually including ministers of finance.

4. Inflation Ultimately Increases Unemployment

But why all this fear of inflation? Should we not try to learn to live with it, as some South American states seem to have done, particularly if, as some believe, this is necessary to secure full employment? If this were true and the harm done by inflation were only that which many people emphasize, we would have to consider this possibility seriously.

Why we cannot live with inflation

The answer, however, is twofold. First, such inflation, in order to achieve the goal aimed at, would have to *accelerate* constantly, and accelerating inflation would sooner or later reach a degree that makes all effective order of a market economy impossible. Second, and more important, in the long run such inflation inevitably creates much *more* unemployment than the amount it was originally designed to prevent.

The argument is often advanced that inflation merely produces a *redistribution* of the social product, while unemployment *reduces* it and therefore represents a worse evil. This argument is false, because *inflation becomes the cause of increased unemployment.*

Harmful effects of inflation

I certainly do not wish to underestimate the other harmful effects of inflation. They are much worse than anyone can conceive who has not lived through a great inflation: During my first eight months in a job, my salary rose to 200 times the initial amount. I am indeed convinced that such a mismanagement of the currency is tolerated only because nobody has the time or energy during an inflation to organize a popular rebellion.

I want to stress that even the effects every citizen experiences are not the worst consequences of inflation; this is usually not understood because *it becomes visible only when the inflation is past.* This must particularly be said to economists, politicians, or others who like to point to the South American countries that have had inflations lasting through several generations and seem to have learned to live with them. In these predominantly agrarian countries, the effects of inflation are chiefly limited to those mentioned. The most serious effects that inflation produces in the labor markets of industrial countries are of minor importance in South America.

The attempts made in some of these countries, Brazil in particular, to deal with the problems of inflation by some method of indexing can, at best, remedy some of the consequences but certainly not the chief causes or the most harmful effects. They cannot prevent the worst damage that inflation causes—the misdirection of labor, a subject I must now consider more fully.

The misdirection of labor

Inflation makes certain jobs *temporarily* attractive. These jobs will disappear when inflation stops, or even when it ceases to accelerate fast enough. This result follows because inflation (a) changes the distribution of the money stream between the various sectors and stages of the process of production, and (b) creates expectation of a further rise in prices.

The defenders of a monetary full-employment policy often represent the position as if a *single* increase of total demand were sufficient to secure full employment for an indefinite but fairly long period. This argument overlooks the inevitable effects of such a policy, both on the distribution of labor among industries and on the wage policy of the trade unions.

As soon as government assumes the responsibility for maintaining full employment at whatever wages the trade unions succeed in obtaining, the latter no longer have any reason to take into account the unemployment their wage demands might have caused. In this situation every rise of wages that exceeds the increase in productivity will make necessary an increase in total

12

demand if unemployment is not to ensue. The increase in the quantity of money made necessary by the upward movement of wages thus released becomes a *continuous* process requiring a constant influx of additional quantities of money.

The additional money supply must lead to changes in the relative strength of demand for various kinds of goods and services. And these changes in relative demand must lead to further changes in relative prices and consequent changes in the direction of production and the allocation of the factors of production, including labor. I must leave aside here all the other reasons why the prices of different goods—and the quantities produced—will react differently to changes in the demand (such as elasticities—the speed with which supply can respond to demand).

The chief conclusion I want to demonstrate is that the longer the inflation lasts, the larger will be the number of workers whose jobs depend on a *continuation* of the inflation, often even on a continuing *acceleration* of the rate of inflation—not because they would not have found employment without the inflation, but because they were drawn by the inflation into *temporarily* attractive jobs, which after a slowing down or cessation of the inflation, will again disappear.

The consequences are unavoidable

We ought to have no illusion that we can escape the consequences of the mistakes we have made. Any attempt to preserve the jobs made profitable by inflation would lead to a complete destruction of the market order. We have once again in the postwar period missed the opportunity to forestall a depression while there was still time to do so. We have in fact used our emancipation from institutional restraints—the gold standard and fixed exchange rates—to act more stupidly than ever before.

But if we cannot escape the reappearance of substantial unemployment, this is not the effect of a failure of "capitalism" or the market economy, but the exclusive consequence of our own errors—errors that past experience and available knowledge ought to have enabled us to avoid. It is unfortunately only too true that the disappointment of expectations they have created

13

may lead to serious social unrest. But this does not mean that we can avoid it. The most serious danger now is that attempts, so attractive for the politicians, to postpone the evil day and thereby make things even worse in the long run, may still succeed. I must confess I have been wishing for some time that the inescapable crisis would come soon. And I hope now that any attempts made to promptly restart the process of monetary expansion will not succeed and that we are forced to choose a new policy.

Temporary, not mass, unemployment

Let me emphasize, however, that although I regard a period of some months, perhaps even more than a year, of considerable unemployment as unavoidable, this does not mean that we must expect another long period of mass unemployment comparable to the Great Depression of the 1930s—provided we do not commit very bad mistakes in policy. Such a development can be prevented by a sensible policy that does not repeat the errors responsible for the duration of the Great Depression.

Before I turn to what our future policy ought to be, I want to reject emphatically a misrepresentation of my point of view. I certainly do not recommend unemployment as a *means* to combat inflation. But my advice is being given at a time when the choice open to us is solely between some unemployment in the near future and more unemployment at a later date. What I fear above all is the *après moi le déluge* attitude of the politicians, who in their concern about the next elections, are likely to opt for more unemployment later. Unfortunately even some commentators, such as the writers of *The Economist*, argue in a similar manner and have called for "reflation" when the increase in the quantity of money is still continuing.

5. What Can Be Done Now?

The first step

The first necessity now is to stop the increase in the quantity of money—or at least to reduce it to the rate of the real growth of production—and this cannot happen soon enough. Moreover, I can see no advantage in a gradual deceleration, although for purely technical reasons, it may be all we can achieve.

It does not follow that we should not endeavor to stop a real deflation when it threatens to set in. Although I do not regard deflation as the original cause of a decline in business activity, a disappointment of expectations unquestionably tends to induce a process of deflation—what more than forty years ago I called a "secondary deflation."[3] Its effect may be worse (and in the 1930s certainly was worse) than warranted by the original cause of the reaction; moreover, it performs no steering function.

I must confess that forty years ago I argued differently. I have since altered my opinion—not about the theoretical explanation of the events, but about the practical possibility of removing the obstacles to the functioning of the system by allowing deflation to proceed for a while.

I then believed that a short period of deflation might modify the rigidity of money wages (what economists have since come to call their "rigidity downwards"), or the resistance to the reduction of some particular money wages, and that in this way we could restore relative wages determined by the market. This still seems an indispensable condition if the market mechanism is to

---

[3] Defined and discussed in Part III, p. 40. I recall that the phrase was frequently used in the London School of Economics Seminar in the 1930s.

function satisfactorily. But I no longer believe it is possible to achieve it in this manner. I probably should have seen then that the last chance was lost when the British government in 1931 abandoned the attempt to bring costs down by deflation just when it seemed near success.

Prevent recession from degenerating into depression

If I were today responsible for the monetary policy of a country, I would certainly try to prevent an impending deflation (that is, an absolute decrease of the stream of incomes) by all suitable means, and would announce that I intended to do so. This alone would probably be sufficient to prevent a degeneration of the recession into a long-lasting depression.

The reestablishment of a properly functioning market would, however, still require a restructuring of the whole system of relative prices and wages, and a readjustment to the expectation of stable prices, which presupposes a much greater flexibility of wages than now exists. What chance we have to achieve such a determination of relative wage-rates by the market and how long it may take, I dare not predict. But although I recognize that a *general* reduction of money wages is politically unachievable, I am still convinced that the required adjustment of the structure of *relative* wages can be achieved without inflation only through the reduction of the money wages of some groups of workers, and therefore must be thus achieved.

From a longer point of view, it is obvious that once we have got over the immediate difficulties, we must not again avail ourselves of the seemingly cheap and easy method of achieving full employment by aiming at the maximum of employment that can in the short run be achieved by monetary pressure.

The Keynesian dream

The Keynesian dream is gone, even though its ghost will continue to plague politics for decades. It is to be wished, although this is clearly too much to hope for, that the term "full employment" itself, which has become so closely associated with the inflationist policy, could be abandoned—or that we should at least remember that it was the aim of classical economists long before Keynes. John Stuart Mill reports in his autobiography how "full employment with high wages" appeared to him in his youth as the chief *desideratum* of economic policy.[4]

Primary aim: stable money, not unstable "full employment"

What we must now be clear about is that our aim must be, not the maximum of employment that can be achieved in the short run, but a "high and stable [i.e., *continuing*] level of employment," as one of the wartime British White Papers on employment policy phrased it.[5] We can achieve this, however, only through the reestablishment of a properly functioning market which, by the free play of prices and wages, establishes the correspondence of supply and demand for each sector.

Though monetary policy must prevent wide fluctuations in the quantity of money or in the volume of the income stream, the effect on employment must not be its dominating consideration. *The primary aim must again become the stability of the value of money.* The currency authorities must again be effectively protected against the political pressure that today forces them so often to take measures that are politically advantageous in the short run but harmful to the community in the long run.

Disciplining the monetary authorities

I wish I could share the confidence of my friend Milton Friedman, who thinks that in order to prevent the abuse of their powers for political purposes, one could deprive the monetary authorities of all discretionary powers by prescribing the amount of money they may and should add to circulation in any one year. Perhaps he regards this as practicable because, for statistical purposes, he has become accustomed to drawing a sharp distinction between what is to be regarded as money and what is not. This distinction does not exist in the real world.

---

[4] J. S. Mill, *Autobiography and Other Writings,* ed. J. Stillinger (Boston: Houghton Mifflin, 1969).

[5] *Employment Policy,* Cmd. 6527 (London: HMSO, May 1944), Foreword.

I believe that to ensure the convertibility of all kinds of near-money into real money, which is necessary if we are to avoid severe liquidity crises or panics, the monetary authorities must be given some discretion. But I agree with Friedman that we will have to try to get back to a more or less automatic system for regulating the quantity of money in ordinary times. His principle is one that monetary authorities ought to aim at, not one to which they ought to be tied by law. The necessity of "suspending" Sir Robert Peel's Bank Act of 1844 three times within twenty-five years after it was passed ought to have taught us this once and for all.

And although I am not as optimistic as the editor of the London *Times,* Mr. William Rees-Mogg, who in a sensational article[6] (and now in a book[7]) has proposed the return to the gold standard, it does make me feel somewhat more optimistic when I see such a proposal coming from so influential a source. I would even agree that among the feasible monetary systems, the international gold standard is the best, if I could believe that the most important countries could be trusted to obey the rules of the game necessary for its preservation. But this seems exceedingly unlikely, and no single country can, on its own, have an effective gold standard. By its nature the gold standard is an international system and can function only as an international system.

It is, however, a big step in the direction of a return to reason when, at the end of his book, Mr. Rees-Mogg argues that

> we should be tearing up the full employment commitment of the 1944 White Paper, a great political and economic revolution.
>   This would until very recently have seemed a high price to pay; now it is no great price at all. There is little or no prospect of maintaining full employment with the present inflation, in Britain or in the world. The full employment standard became a commitment to inflation, but the inflation has now accelerated past the point at which it is compatible with full employment.[8]

[6] "Crisis of Paper Currencies: Has the Time Come for Britain to Return to the Gold Standard?" *Times* (London), 1 May 1974.

[7] William Rees-Mogg, *The Reigning Error: The Crisis of World Inflation* (London: Hamish Hamilton, 1974).

[8] Ibid., p. 112.

Equally encouraging is a statement of the British Chancellor of the Exchequer, Mr. Denis Healey, who is reported to have said:

> It is far better that more people should be in work, *even if that means accepting lower wages on average,* than that those lucky enough to keep their jobs should scoop the pool while millions are living on the dole.[9] (Italics added.)

It would almost seem as if in Britain, the country in which the harmful doctrines originated, a reversal of opinion were now under way. Let us hope it will rapidly spread over the world.

[9]Speech at East Leeds Labour Club, reported in the *Times* (London), 11 January 1975.

PART II.
The Pretense of Knowledge

The Pretense of Knowledge

The particular occasion of this lecture, combined with the chief practical problem that economists have to face today, has made the choice of topic almost inevitable. On the one hand, the recent establishment of the Nobel Prize in Economic Science marks a significant step in the process by which, in the opinion of the general public, economics has been conceded some of the dignity and prestige of the physical sciences. On the other hand, economists are at this moment being called upon to extricate the free world from the serious threat of accelerating inflation, which— it must be admitted—was brought about by policies the majority of economists recommended and even urged governments to pursue. We have indeed at the moment little cause for pride: As a profession we have made a mess of things.

The "scientistic" attitude*

It seems to me that this failure of economists to guide policy more successfully is closely connected with their propensity to imitate as closely as possible the procedures of the brilliantly successful physical sciences—an attempt that in our subject may lead to outright error. It is an approach that has come to be described as the "scientistic" attitude, which, as I defined it some thirty years ago,

> is decidedly unscientific in the true sense of the word, since it involves a mechanical and uncritical application of habits of thought to fields different from those in which they have been formed.[1]

*[The subheadings have been inserted to help readers, especially those unfamiliar with Professor Hayek's writings, to follow the argument; they were not part of the original Nobel Lecture. —ED.]

[1] "Scientism and the Study of Society," *Economica,* August 1942, reprinted in *The Counter-Revolution of Science* (Glencoe, Ill.: Free Press, 1952), p. 15.

I want to begin by explaining how some of the gravest errors of recent economic policy are a direct consequence of this scientistic error.

The theory that has been guiding monetary and financial policy for the past thirty years—a theory I contend is largely the product of a mistaken conception of the proper scientific procedure—rests on the assertion that there exists a simple positive correlation between total employment and the size of the aggregate demand for goods and services; and it leads to the belief that we can permanently ensure full employment by maintaining total money expenditure at an appropriate level. Among the various theories advanced to account for extensive unemployment, this is probably the only one that can be supported by strong quantitative evidence. I nevertheless regard it as fundamentally false, and to act upon it, as we now realize, is very harmful.

This brings me to the crucial issue—the difference between economics and the physical sciences. In economics (and in other disciplines that deal with what I call "essentially complex" phenomena), we can obtain quantitative data for only certain aspects of the events to be explained, and this necessarily limited number may not include the important aspects. While in the physical sciences it is generally assumed, probably with good reason, that any important factor that determines the observed events will itself be directly observable and measurable, in the study of such "essentially complex" phenomena as the market, which depend on the actions of many individuals, all the circumstances that will determine the outcome of a process, for reasons I shall explain later, *will hardly ever be fully known or measurable.* And while in the physical sciences the investigator will be able to measure, on the basis of a *prima facie* theory, what he thinks important, in the social sciences what is treated as important is often that which happens to be accessible to measurement. This is sometimes carried to the point where it is demanded that our theories must be formulated in such terms that they refer only to measurable magnitudes.

It can hardly be denied that such a demand quite arbitrarily limits the facts that are to be admitted as possible causes of the events in the real world. This view, which is often quite naively

24

accepted as required by scientific procedure, has some rather paradoxical consequences. We know, of course, about the market and similar social structures, very many facts that we cannot measure and on which indeed we have only some very imprecise and general information. And because the effects of these facts in any particular instance cannot be confirmed by quantitative evidence, they are simply disregarded by those sworn to accept only what they regard as scientific evidence. And they thereupon happily proceed on the fiction that the factors they can measure are the only relevant ones.

The correlation between aggregate demand and total employment, for instance, may be only approximate; but as it is the *only* one on which we have quantitative data, it is accepted as the only causal connection that counts. On this standard there may well exist better "scientific" evidence for a false theory, which will be accepted because it appears as more "scientific," than for a valid explanation, which is rejected because there is not sufficient quantitative evidence for it.

The chief cause of unemployment

Let me illustrate this by a brief account of what I regard as the chief true cause of extensive unemployment—an account that will also explain why such unemployment cannot be cured permanently by the inflationary policies recommended by the theory now fashionable. The correct explanation appears to me to be the existence of discrepancies between the distribution of demand among the different goods and services, and the allocation of labor and other resources among the production of those outputs. We possess a fairly good qualitative knowledge of the forces by which a correspondence between demand and supply in the different sectors of the economic system is brought about, of the conditions under which it will be achieved, and of the factors likely to prevent such an adjustment. The separate steps in the account of this process rely on facts of everyday experience, and few who follow the argument will question the validity of the factual assumptions or the logical correctness of the conclusions

25

drawn from them. We have good reason to believe that unemployment indicates that the structure of *relative* prices and wages has been distorted (usually by monopolistic or governmental price-fixing), and that to restore equality between the demand for and the supply of labor in all sectors, changes of relative prices and wages and some transfers of labor will be necessary.

But when we are asked for quantitative evidence for the particular structure of prices and wages that would be required to assure a smooth continuous sale of the products and services offered, we must admit that we have no such information. We know, in other words, the general conditions in which what we call, somewhat misleadingly, an "equilibrium" will establish itself, but we never know the particular prices or wages that would exist if the market were to bring about such an equilibrium. We can merely say under which conditions we can expect the market to establish prices and wages at which demand will equal supply. But we can never produce statistical information that would show how much the prevailing prices and wages *deviate* from those that would secure a continuous sale of the current supply of labor. This account of the causes of unemployment is an empirical theory, in the sense that it might be proved false—if, for example, with a constant money supply, a general increase of wages did not lead to unemployment. But it is certainly not the kind of theory we could use to obtain specific numerical predictions concerning the rates of wages, or the distribution of labor, to be expected.

Why should we in economics, however, have to plead ignorance of the sort of facts on which, in the case of a physical theory, a scientist would certainly be expected to give precise information? (It is probably not surprising that people impressed by the example of the physical sciences should find this position very unsatisfactory and should insist on the standards of proof they find there.) The reason for this state of affairs, as I have briefly indicated, is that the social sciences, like much of biology but unlike most of the physical sciences, have to deal with structures of *essential* complexity, that is, structures whose characteristic properties can be exhibited only by models made up of relatively large numbers of variables. Competition, for example, is a process that will produce certain results only if it proceeds among a fairly *large* number of acting persons.

In some inquiries, particularly where problems of a similar kind arise in the physical sciences, the difficulties can be overcome by using, not specific information about the individual elements, but data about the relative frequency, or the probability, of the occurrence of the various distinctive properties of the elements. But this is true only where we have to deal with what Dr. Warren Weaver distinguishes with admirable precision as "phenomena of unorganized complexity," in contrast to those "phenomena of organized complexity" with which we have to deal in the social sciences.[2] Organized complexity here means that the character of the structures evincing it depends not only on the properties of the individual elements of which they are composed, and the relative frequency with which they occur, but also on the manner in which the individual elements are connected with one another. Thus in explaining the working of such structures, we cannot replace the information about the individual elements by statistical information; we must have full information about each element if from our theory we are to derive specific predictions about individual events. Without such specific information about the individual elements, we shall be confined to what on another occasion I have called mere "pattern predictions"—predictions of some of the general attributes of the structures that will form themselves, but not containing specific statements about the individual elements of which the structures will be made up.[3]

This is particularly true of our theories accounting for the determination of the systems of relative prices and wages that will form themselves on a well-functioning market. Into the deter-

[2]Warren Weaver, "A Quarter Century in the Natural Sciences," in *The Rockefeller Foundation Annual Report* (New York, 1958), chap. 1, "Science and Complexity."

[3]See my essay, "The Theory of Complex Phenomena," in *The Critical Approach to Science and Philosophy: Essays in Honor of K. R. Popper,* ed. M. Bunge (New York, 1964). Reprinted (with additions) in my *Studies in Philosophy, Politics and Economics* (Chicago: University of Chicago Press; London: Routledge & Kegan Paul, 1967).

mination of these prices and wages will enter the effects of particular information possessed by every one of the participants in the market process, a sum of facts that in their totality cannot be known to the scientific observer or to any other single brain. It is indeed the source of the superiority of the market order (and the reason why, so long as it is not suppressed by the powers of government, it regularly displaces other types of order) that in the resulting allocation of resources, it uses more of the knowledge of particular facts—knowledge that is dispersed among uncounted persons—than any one person can possess. But because we, the observing scientists, can never *know* all the determinants of such an order, and in consequence cannot know at which particular structure of prices and wages demand would everywhere equal supply, we also cannot measure the deviations from that order. Nor can we statistically test our theory that it is the deviations from that "equilibrium" system of prices and wages that make it impossible to sell certain products and services at the prices at which they are offered.

Mathematical method in economics: uses and limitations

Before exploring the effects of all this on the employment policies currently pursued, allow me to define more specifically the inherent limitations, so often overlooked, of our numerical knowledge. I want to do this to avoid giving the impression that I generally reject the mathematical method in economics. I regard it indeed as the great advantage of the mathematical technique that it allows us to describe, by algebraic equations, the general character of a pattern even where we are ignorant of the numerical values determining its particular manifestation. Without this algebraic technique we could scarcely have achieved that comprehensive picture of the *mutual interdependencies* of the different events in a market. It has, however, led to the illusion that we can use this technique to determine and predict the *numerical values* of those magnitudes; and this has led to a vain search for quantitative or numerical constants.

This happened despite the fact that the modern founders of mathematical economics had no such illusions. It is true that their systems of equations describing the pattern of a market equilibrium are so framed that *if* we were able to fill in all the blanks of the abstract formulae—that is, *if* we knew all the parameters of those equations—we could calculate the prices and quantities of all commodities and services sold. But, as clearly stated by Vilfredo Pareto, one of the founders of this theory, its purpose cannot be "to arrive at a numerical calculation of prices" because, as he said, it would be "absurd" to assume that we could ascertain all the data.[4] Indeed, the chief point was seen by those remarkable anticipators of modern economics, the Spanish Schoolmen of the sixteenth century, who emphasized that what they called *pretium mathematicum,* the mathematical price, depended on so many particular circumstances that it could never be known to man but was known only to God.[5]

I sometimes wish that our mathematical economists would take this to heart. I must confess that I still doubt whether their search for measurable magnitudes has made significant contributions to our *theoretical understanding* of economic phenomena, as distinct from a *description* of particular situations. Nor am I prepared to accept the excuse that this branch of research is still very young: Sir William Petty, the founder of econometrics, was, after all, a somewhat senior colleague of Sir Isaac Newton in the Royal Society!

There may be few instances in which the superstition that only measurable magnitudes can be important has done positive harm in the economic field. But the present problem of inflation and employment is a very serious instance: What is generally the true cause of extensive unemployment has been disregarded by the scientistically-minded majority of economists, because its operation could not be confirmed by directly observable relations between measurable magnitudes. Instead, an almost exclusive concentration on quantitatively measurable surface phenomena has produced a policy that has made matters worse.

[4] V. Pareto, *Manuel d'économie politique,* 2d ed. (Paris, 1927), pp. 223-24.

[5] See, for example, Luis Molina, *De iustitia et iure,* tom. II (Cologne, 1596-1600), disp. 347, no. 3; and particularly Johannes de Lugo, *Disputationum de iustitia et iure,* tom. II (Lyon, 1642), disp. 26, sect. 4, no. 40.

Admittedly, the kind of theory I regard as the true explanation of unemployment has its limitations because it allows us to make only very general predictions of the *kind* of events we must expect in a given situation, but the effects on policy of the more ambitious constructions have not been very fortunate. I confess that I prefer true but imperfect knowledge, even if it leaves much undetermined and unpredictable, to a pretense of exact knowledge that is likely to be false. The credit gained for seemingly simple but false theories by their apparent conformity with recognized scientific standards may, as the present instance shows, have grave consequences.

Indeed, in the case discussed, the very measure that the dominant "macroeconomic" theory has recommended as a remedy for unemployment, namely the increase of aggregate demand, has become a cause of a very extensive misallocation of resources that is likely to make later large-scale unemployment inevitable. The continuous injection of additional amounts of money into the economic system at points where it creates a temporary demand—a demand that must cease when the increase of the quantity of money stops or slows down—together with the expectation of a continuing rise of prices, draws labor and other resources into employment that can last only as long as the increase of the quantity of money continues at the same rate—or perhaps only as long as it continues to accelerate at a given rate.

What this policy has produced is not so much a level of employment that could not have been brought about in other ways, but a distribution of employment that cannot be maintained indefinitely and that, after some time, can be maintained only by a rate of inflation that would rapidly lead to a disorganization of all economic activity. As the result of a mistaken theoretical view, we have been led into a precarious position in which we cannot prevent substantial unemployment from reappearing; not because this unemployment is deliberately brought about as a means to combat inflation (as my view is sometimes misrepresented), but because it is now bound to occur as a regrettable but *inescapable* consequence of the mistaken policies of the past as soon as inflation ceases to accelerate.

I have introduced these problems of immediate practical importance chiefly to illustrate the momentous consequences that may follow from errors concerning abstract problems of the philosophy of science. There is as much reason to be apprehensive about the long-run dangers created in a much wider field by the uncritical acceptance of assertions that have the *appearance* of being scientific.

When science is unscientific

What I mainly wanted to show by the topical illustration is that—certainly in my subject, but also generally in the sciences of man—what looks superficially like the most scientific procedure is often the most unscientific, and, beyond this, that in these other activities there are definite limits to what we can expect science to achieve. To entrust to science—or to deliberate control according to scientific principles—more than scientific method can achieve may have deplorable effects. The progress of the natural sciences in modern times has, of course, so much exceeded all expectations that any suggestion that there may be some limits to it is bound to arouse suspicion.

This insight will be especially resisted by all who have hoped that our increasing power of prediction and control, generally attributed to scientific advance, when applied to the processes of society, would soon enable us to mold society entirely to our liking. It is indeed true that, in contrast to the exhilaration that the discoveries of the physical sciences tend to produce, the insights we gain from the study of society more often have a dampening effect on our aspirations; and it is perhaps not surprising that the more impetuous younger members of our profession are not always prepared to accept this truth. Yet the confidence in the unlimited power of science is only too often based on a false belief that the scientific method consists in the application of a ready-made technique, or in imitating the form rather than the substance of scientific procedure, as if one needed only to follow some cookbook recipes to solve all social problems. It sometimes seems almost as if the *techniques* of science were more easily learned than the *thinking* that shows us what the problems are and how to approach them.

31

The conflict between what the public, in its present mood, expects science to achieve in satisfaction of popular hopes and what is really in its power is a serious matter. Even if all true scientists recognized the limitations of what they can do in human affairs, so long as the public expects more, there will always be some who will pretend, and perhaps honestly believe, that they can do more to meet popular demands than is really in their power. It is often difficult enough for the expert, and certainly in many instances impossible for the layman, to distinguish between justified and unjustified claims advanced in the name of science. For example, the enormous publicity given by the media to a report expounding in the name of science on *The Limits to Growth,* and the silence of the same media about the devastating criticism this report has received from competent experts,[6] must make one feel somewhat apprehensive about the use to which the prestige of science can be put.

But it is by no means only in economics that far-reaching claims are made for a more scientific direction of all human activities and the desirability of replacing spontaneous processes by "conscious human control." If I am not mistaken, psychology, psychiatry, some branches of sociology, and still more the so-called philosophy of history are even more affected by what I have called the scientistic prejudice and by specious claims as to what science can achieve.[7]

If we are to safeguard the reputation of science and prevent the misappropriation of knowledge based on a superficial similarity of procedure with that of the physical sciences, much effort will have to be directed toward debunking such misappropria-

[6]D. L. Meadows and D. H. Meadows, eds., *The Limits to Growth: A Report for the Club of Rome's Project on the Predicament of Mankind* (New York, 1972). For a systematic examination of this document by a distinguished economist, see Wilfred Beckerman, *In Defence of Economic Growth* (London, 1974). For a list of earlier criticisms by experts, see Gottfried Haberler, *Economic Growth and Stability* (Los Angeles, 1974), who rightly calls their effect "devastating."

[7]For some illustrations of these tendencies in other subjects, see my inaugural lecture as Visiting Professor at the University of Salzburg, *Die Irrtümer des Konstruktivismus und die Grundlagen legitimer Kritik gesellschaftlicher Gebilde* (Munich, 1970) now reissued for the Walter Eucken Institute at Freiburg im Breisgau (Tübingen: J. C. B. Mohr, 1975).

tions, some of which have by now become the vested interests of established university departments. We cannot be grateful enough to such modern philosophers of science as Sir Karl Popper for giving us a test by which we can distinguish between what we may and may not accept as scientific—a test that some doctrines now widely accepted as scientific would surely not pass.

Such essentially complex phenomena as social structures, however, pose special problems that prompt me to restate in more general terms the reasons why in these fields not only are there absolute obstacles to the prediction of specific events, but also why to act as if we possessed scientific knowledge enabling us to transcend them may itself become a serious obstacle to the advance of the human intellect.

Obstacles to prediction

The chief point we must remember is that the vast and rapid advance of the physical sciences took place in fields where explanation and prediction could be based on laws that accounted for the observed phenomena as functions of comparatively *few* variables—either particular facts or relative frequencies of events. This may even be the ultimate reason we single out these realms as "physical" in contrast to those more highly organized structures I have here called "essentially complex" phenomena. There is no reason for the situation to be the same in the latter as in the former fields. The difficulties we encounter with essentially complex phenomena do not, as one might at first suspect, concern the formulation of theories to explain the observed events—although essentially complex phenomena do entail special difficulties in testing proposed explanations and therefore in eliminating bad theories. The chief problem that arises when we apply our theories to any particular situation in the real world is that a theory of essentially complex phenomena must refer to a *large* number of particular facts, all of which must be ascertained before we can derive a prediction from it, or test it.

Once we succeed in this task, there should be no particular difficulty about deriving testable predictions. With the help of modern computers, it should be easy enough to insert these data into the appropriate blanks of the theoretical formulae and to derive a prediction. The real difficulty, to the solution of which science has *little* to contribute and which is sometimes indeed *insoluble,* consists of the ascertainment of the particular facts.

A simple example will show the nature of this difficulty. Consider a ball game played by a few people of approximately equal skill. If, in addition to our general knowledge of the ability of the individual players, we knew a few particular facts such as their state of attention, their perceptions, and the state of their hearts, lungs, muscles, etc., at each moment of the game, we could probably predict the outcome. Indeed, if we were familiar both with the game and the teams, we would probably have a fairly shrewd idea about what the outcome would depend on. But we would not, of course, be able to ascertain those facts, and so the result of the game would be outside the range of the scientifically predictable, however well we might know what effects particular events would have on the result of the game. This does not mean that we could make no predictions at all about the course of the game. If we know the rules of the different games, we shall, in watching one, very soon know which game is being played and what kinds of actions we can and cannot expect. But our capacity to predict will be confined to such *general* characteristics of the events to be expected, and will not include the capacity of predicting *particular* individual events.

This explanation corresponds to what I have called earlier the mere pattern predictions to which we are increasingly confined as we move from the realm where relatively simple laws prevail into the range of phenomena where organized complexity rules. As we advance, we find more and more frequently that we can in practice ascertain some, but not all, of the particular circumstances that determine the outcome of a given process. In consequence, we are able to predict some, but not all, of the properties of the result we have to expect. Often all we shall be able to predict will be some abstract characteristic of the pattern that will appear—relations between kinds of elements about which individually we know very little. Yet, as I am anxious to repeat, we will still achieve predictions that can be falsified and that therefore satisfy Popper's test of empirical significance.

Of course, compared with the precise predictions we have learned to expect in the physical sciences, this sort of mere pattern prediction is a second best. Yet the danger against which I want to warn is precisely the belief that it is necessary to achieve more in order to claim to be accepted as scientific. This way lies charlatanism, and worse. To act on the belief that we possess the knowledge and the power that enable us to shape the processes of society entirely to our liking, knowledge that in the real world we do *not* possess, is likely to make us do much harm.

Power to coerce may impede spontaneous forces

In the physical sciences there may be little objection to trying to do the impossible; we might even feel that we ought not to discourage the overconfident because their experiments may, after all, produce new insights. But in the social sciences, the erroneous belief that the exercise of some power would have beneficial consequences is likely to lead to bestowing on some authority a new power to *coerce* others. Even if such power is not in itself bad, its exercise is likely to impede the functioning of those spontaneous ordering forces by which, without understanding them, man is, in the real world, so largely assisted in the pursuit of his aims.

We are only beginning to understand on how subtle a communications system the functioning of an advanced industrial society is based. This communications system, which we call the market, turns out to be a more efficient mechanism for digesting dispersed information than any that man has deliberately designed.

If man is not to do more harm than good in his efforts to improve the social order, he will have to learn that in this, as in all other fields where essential complexity of an organized kind prevails, *he cannot acquire the full knowledge that would make mastery of the events possible.* He will therefore have to use what knowledge he can achieve, not to shape the results as the craftsman shapes his handiwork, but rather to cultivate growth by providing the appropriate environment, as the gardener does for his plants.

35

There is danger in the exuberant feeling of ever growing power, engendered by the advance of the physical sciences, which tempts man to try—"dizzy with success," to use a characteristic phrase of early communism—to subject not only our natural but also our human environment to the control of human will. The recognition of the insuperable limits to his knowledge ought indeed to teach the student of society a lesson of humility that should keep him from becoming an accomplice in man's fatal striving to control society—a striving that makes him not only a tyrant over his fellows, but may well make him destroy a civilization that no brain has designed, a civilization that has grown from the free efforts of millions of individuals.

PART III.
Unemployment: Inevitable Consequence of Inflation

Unemployment: Inevitable Consequence of Inflation

The primary duty today of any economist who deserves the name seems to me to stress, at every opportunity, the fact that the present unemployment is the direct and inevitable consequence of the so-called full-employment policies pursued for the past twenty-five years. Most people still mistakenly believe that an increase in aggregate demand will eliminate unemployment for some time. Nothing short of the realization that this remedy, though usually effective in the short run, produces much more unemployment later, will prevent the public from exerting irresistible pressure to resume inflation as soon as unemployment increases substantially.

To understand this basic truth is to recognize that the majority of economists whose advice governments have been following everywhere in Britain and the rest of the Western world during this period have thoroughly discredited themselves and ought to do penance in sackcloth and ashes. What was almost unquestioned orthodoxy for close to thirty years has been thoroughly discredited. And the economic crisis also marks a severe setback in the authority of economics—or at least marks the long-overdue collapse of the fashionable Keynesian doctrine that has dominated opinion for a generation. I am fully convinced that before we can hope to return to reasonable stability, not to mention lasting prosperity, we must exorcise the Keynesian incubus. By this I mean not so much what John Maynard Keynes himself taught—because you can find in Keynes, as in Marx, almost anything—but rather the teaching of those Keynesians who, as Professor Joan Robinson recently wrote, "sometimes had some trouble in getting Maynard to see what the point of his revolution really was."[1]

Keynes confirmed business's belief in high demand

The conquest of opinion by Keynesian economics is due mainly to the fact that its argument conformed to the age-old belief of the businessman that his prosperity depended on consumer demand. This plausible but erroneous conclusion was derived from his individual experience in business, namely, that general prosperity could be maintained by keeping general demand high. Economic theory had been rejecting this conclusion for generations, but it was suddenly made respectable again by Keynes. And since the 1930s it has been embraced as obvious good sense by a whole generation of economists brought up on the teaching of his school. Thus for a quarter of a century we have systematically employed all available methods of increasing money expenditure, which in the short run creates additional employment but at the same time leads to misdirections of labor that must ultimately result in extensive unemployment.

"Secondary depression" and monetary countermeasures

This fundamental connection between inflation and unemployment is obscured because, although insufficient demand is normally *not* the primary cause of unemployment—except during an actual deflation, i.e., a decrease in the quantity of money— unemployment may itself become the cause of an absolute shrinkage of aggregate demand. This in turn may bring about a further increase of unemployment and thus lead to a cumulative process of contraction in which unemployment feeds on unemployment. Such a "secondary depression" caused by an induced deflation should of course be prevented by appropriate monetary countermeasures. (The difficult question, which I can mention only briefly here, is how this can be done without pro-

---

[1] Joan Robinson, "What Has Become of the Keynesian Revolution?" in *Essays on John Maynard Keynes,* ed. Milo Keynes (Cambridge: At the University Press, 1975), p. 125.

ducing further misdirections of labor.) At this moment, however, our chief task is still to prevent the resort to a renewed spurt of inflation in an effort to combat the unemployment made inevitable through misdirections of labor. Such a course would only increase these misdirections and thus make matters worse in the long run.

Difficult to discover the misdirected labor in the "long prosperity"

A short exposition cannot do justice to the complexity of the facts in another important problem: In the booms-followed-by-depressions of the past, the misdirections of labor were comparatively easy to trace because the expansion of credit during the boom served industrial investment almost exclusively. But during the long postwar period of prosperity, which was maintained by removing the automatic checks on continued inflation (e.g., the gold standard, fixed exchange rates), by relieving deficit countries of the necessity to contract their money supply, and by providing extra international liquidity, the additional demand financed by inflation was much more widely dispersed and is therefore much more difficult to trace. Its effect on the allocation of resources in general, and especially of labor, would have to be investigated separately for each country and each part of the period—and I am by no means clear as to where the most important overdevelopments would be found. The places where the misplaced, and in consequence now *dis*placed, workers can find lasting employment can be discovered only by letting the market operate freely.

Recovery must come from a revival of profitable investment

In general it is probably true to say that a *temporary* "full employment" position might be approached if, by providing employment through public works (from which workers will wish to move as soon as they can to other and better-paid positions), consumer demand is prevented from falling substantially. To directly stimulate investment and similar expenditure, however, will only draw workers into jobs that they will expect to be permanent but that will end as soon as the source of this expenditure dries up.

41

We must certainly expect the recovery to come from a revival of investment. But we want investment of the kind that will prove profitable and can be continued when a new position of fair stability and high-level employment has been achieved. Neither subsidization of investment nor artificially low interest rates is likely to achieve this position. And least of all is the desirable (i.e., stable) form of investment to be brought about by stimulating consumer demand.

Part of the same widespread fallacy, to which the businessman is especially prone, is the belief that in order to make new investment profitable, consumer demand must increase. It is true only in relation to investment designed to increase output by using the *same* techniques as hitherto employed, but it is not true as to the only sort of investment that can increase per capita productivity by supplying a given labor force with *more* capital equipment. Such intensification of capital use is indeed encouraged by relatively *low* product (consumer good) prices—which make it necessary to save on labor costs—and discouraged by high ones. This is one of the elementary connections between wages and investment wholly overlooked in Keynesian economics.

Monetarism and the mechanical (macro) quantity theory

Usually described as the "monetarist" position is the contention that government monetary policy is wholly responsible for the excessive increase in the quantity of money and the consequent general rise in prices experienced throughout the Western world. In this general form, such a position seems to me incontrovertible, even though it is also true that what has led governments to such a policy was chiefly the activity of trade unions, and similar activities of other monopolistic bodies (like the oil cartel). But in a narrower sense, "monetarist" is today frequently used to describe the exponents of a somewhat mechanical form of the quantity theory of the value of money, which in my opinion tends to oversimplify the theoretical argument.

My chief objection to this theory is that, as a "macrotheory," it pays attention only to the effect of changes in the quantity of money on the general price level and not to the effects on the

42

structure of relative prices. Thus it tends to disregard what seem to me the most harmful effects of inflation: the misdirection of resources it causes and the unemployment that ultimately results from it.

Nevertheless, for most practical purposes, this simple form of the quantity theory is a decidedly helpful guide; we should not forget that the great inflations of the past, particularly those in Germany of the early 1920s and the late 1940s, were in effect stopped by men who acted on this somewhat crude form of the quantity theory.[2] But, though this oversimplified explanation of events seems to me inadequate to account for some of the deleterious effects of changes in the quantity of money, I emphasized nearly forty-five years ago, when I attempted to remedy these defects, that "it would be one of the worst things which could befall us if the general public should ever again cease to believe in the elementary propositions of the quantity theory,"[3] which was then represented chiefly by the economists Irving Fisher and Gustav Cassel. But exactly this has happened as the result of the persuasive powers of Lord Keynes, whose proposals for combating the depression of the 1930s had been blocked by the traditional views.

Cantillon and Keynes

The defects of what became the traditional approach had been pointed out 200 years earlier, when Richard Cantillon criticized John Locke's similar mechanical quantity theory, arguing that Locke

> realised well that the abundance of money makes everything dear, but he did not analyse how that takes place. The great difficulty of that analysis consists in the discovery by what path and in what proportion the increase of money raises the price of things.[4]

Cantillon was the first to attempt this analysis. In time the examination of how an inflow of additional money alters the

---

[2] Hjalmar Schacht and Ludwig Erhard respectively.

[3] *Prices and Production* (London: Routledge, 1931), p. 3. E. von Böhm-Bawerk used to speak of "the indestructible core of truth in the quantity theory."

[4] Richard Cantillon, *An Essay on the Nature of Commerce in General,* ed. Henry Higgs (London: Macmillan, 1931), pt. 1, chap. 6.

relative demand for different commodities and services, led to an explanation of how inflation results in a misdirection of resources, particularly of labor, which becomes "redundant" as soon as inflation slows down or even ceases to accelerate. But this promising stream of thought was overwhelmed by the Keynesian flood, which caused a severe retrogression in economics and re-opened the gates to errors of government policy of which our grandparents would have been ashamed.

Governments have acted on poor advice

The present inflation has been deliberately brought about by governments, acting on the advice of economists. As early as 1957 the British Labour Party, in its proposals for a national pension fund, dealt with the problem of future price movements by the assumption that prices would double between 1960 and 1980[5]— then an alarming prospect but now of course already far surpassed. As long ago as 1948 a highly influential economics textbook could plead that a 5 percent per annum increase in prices (which means that prices would double in less than thirteen years) was innocuous.[6] These economists and others overlooked the fact that their goals required an accelerating inflation, and any accelerating inflation sooner or later becomes unbearable. Inflation at a constant rate soon comes to be anticipated in ordinary business transactions; while it does no good, it merely harms the recipients of fixed contractual incomes.

"Inflation": true and false

Much confusion is caused in current discussion by a constant misuse of the term "inflation." Its original and proper meaning is an excessive increase in the quantity of money, leading in turn to an increase in prices. But a general rise in prices, for instance one brought about by a shortage of food caused by bad harvests, is

---

[5]*National Superannuation: Labour's Policy for Security in Old Age* (London: British Labour Party, 1957), pp. 104, 109.

[6]"If price increases could be held down to, say, less than 5 per cent per year, such a mild steady inflation need not cause too great concern." —Paul A. Samuelson, *Economics: An Introductory Analysis* (New York: McGraw-Hill, 1948), p. 282.

not inflation. Nor could we properly call "inflation" a general rise in prices caused by a shortage of oil and other sources of energy that led to an absolute reduction of consumption, unless this shortage had been the pretext for a further increase in the quantity of money. There may also be inflation that considerably harms the working of the market without any rise in prices—if the rise is prevented by controls. Indeed such a "repressed" inflation tends to disorganize economic activity even more than open inflation. Moreover, it has no beneficial effects whatsoever, even in the short run (except for the recipients of the additional money), and leads straight to a centrally directed economy.

No choice between inflation and unemployment

Inflation has, of course, many other bad effects, much more grave and painful than is realized by most people who have not lived through a serious inflation. But the effect that is most devastating, and at the same time the least understood, is that in the long run inflation inevitably produces extensive unemployment. It is simply not true, as some economists have suggested, that as long as unemployment exists, an increase in aggregate demand does only good and no harm. That may be true in the short run but not in the long run. We do not have the choice between inflation and unemployment, just as we cannot choose between overeating and indigestion: Overeating may be very pleasant while we are doing it, but the day of reckoning—the indigestion—is sure to follow.

RECOMMENDED READING

Anderson, Benjamin. *Economics and the Public Welfare: Financial and Economic History of the U.S., 1914–1946.* New York: Van Nostrand, 1949.

———. *The Great Depression.* New York: Macmillan, 1934.

———. *The Value of Money.* New York: Macmillan, 1926.

Baxter, W. T. "The Accountant's Contribution to the Trade Cycle." *Economica,* May 1955, pp. 99–112.

Bresciani-Turroni, Costantino. *The Economics of Inflation: A Study of Currency Depreciation in Post-War Germany.* New York: Kelley, 1976.

Brough, William. *Open Mints and Free Banking.* New York: Putnam, 1894.

Carroll, Charles H. *The Organization of Debt into Currency, and Other Essays.* Princeton, N.J.: Van Nostrand, 1962.

De Roover, Raymond. *Business, Banking, and Economic Thought in Late Medieval and Early Modern Europe.* Chicago: University of Chicago Press, 1974.

Dewey, David R. *Financial History of the United States.* New York: Kelley, 1969.

Farrer, Thomas H. *Studies in Currency, 1898.* New York: Kelley, 1968.

Fetter, Frank A. "Some Neglected Aspects of Gresham's Law." *Quarterly Journal of Economics* 46 (1931–32): 480–95.

Garrett, Garet. *A Bubble That Broke the World.* Boston: Little, Brown, 1932.

Gouge, William M. *A Short History of Paper Money and Banking in the United States.* New York: Kelley, 1968.

Groseclose, Elgin. *Fifty Years of Managed Money: The Story of the Federal Reserve.* New York: Books, Inc., 1966.

————. *Money and Man: A Survey of Monetary Experience.* Norman: University of Oklahoma Press, 1976.

Guttman, Nathan, and Meehan, Patricia. *The Great Inflation: Germany, 1919-1923.* New York: Saxon House, 1975.

Haberler, Gottfried. *Prosperity and Depression: A Theoretical Analysis of Cyclical Movements.* 4th ed., pp. 5-84. Cambridge: Harvard University Press, 1958.

Haberler, G.; Hayek, F. A.; Rothbard, M. N.; and Mises, L. von. *Austrian Theory of the Trade Cycle, and Other Essays.* New York: Center for Libertarian Studies, 1978.

Hawtrey, Ralph G. *The Art of Central Banking.* Clifton, N.J.: Kelley, 1965.

————. *A Century of Bank Rate.* Clifton, N.J.: Kelley, 1965.

Hayek, Friedrich A. *Choice in Currency: A Way to Stop Inflation.* London: Institute of Economic Affairs, 1977.

————. *The Denationalisation of Money.* London: Institute of Economic Affairs, 1976.

————. *Monetary Nationalism and International Stability.* New York: Kelley, 1971.

————. *Monetary Theory and the Trade Cycle.* New York: Kelley, 1975.

————. *New Studies in Philosophy, Politics, Economics, and the History of Ideas,* pp. 165-78, 191-231. Chicago: University of Chicago Press, 1978.

————. *Prices and Production.* New York: Kelley, 1967.

————. *Profits, Interest and Investment, and Other Essays on the Theory of Industrial Fluctuations.* New York: Kelley, 1975.

————. *A Tiger by the Tail: The Keynesian Legacy of Inflation.* San Francisco: Cato Institute, 1979.

Hazlitt, Henry. *The Failure of the "New Economics."* New Rochelle, N.Y.: Arlington House, 1959.

————. *What You Should Know about Inflation.* New York: Funk & Wagnalls, 1968.

————, ed. *The Critics of Keynesian Economics.* New Rochelle, N.Y.: Arlington House, 1977.

Hutt, William H. *The Theory of Idle Resources.* Indianapolis: Liberty Press, 1977.

Jevons, William S. *Money and the Mechanism of Exchange.* London: Kegan Paul, 1905.

Kirzner, Israel M. *The Economic Point of View: An Essay in the History of Economic Thought,* pp. 91-107. Kansas City: Sheed & Ward, 1976.

——. *Perception, Opportunity, and Profit.* Chicago: University of Chicago Press, 1979.

Lachmann, Ludwig M. *Macroeconomic Thinking and the Market Economy.* Menlo Park, Calif.: Institute for Humane Studies, 1978.

Law, John. *Money and Trade Considered.* Clifton, N.J.: Kelley, 1966.

Lindahl, Erik R. *Studies in the Theory of Money and Capital.* New York: Kelley, 1970.

Lutz, Friedrich A. "Essential Properties of a Medium of Exchange." In *Roads to Freedom: Essays in Honour of Friedrich A. Hayek,* edited by E. Streissler, pp. 105-16. London: Routledge & Kegan Paul, 1969.

Machlup, Fritz. *The Stock Market, Credit and Capital Formation.* New York: Macmillan, 1940.

MacManus, T.; Nelson, R.; and Phillips, C. *Banking and the Business Cycle.* New York: Macmillan, 1937.

McGrane, Reginald C. *Foreign Bondholders and American State Debts.* New York: Macmillan, 1935.

Miller, Harry E. *Banking Theories in the United States Before 1860.* New York: Kelley, 1972.

Mises, Ludwig von. *Human Action: A Treatise on Economics,* pp. 398-478, 538-86, 780-803. Chicago: Regnery, 1966.

——. *On the Manipulation of Money and Credit.* Dobbs Ferry, N.Y.: Free Market Books, 1978.

——. *Planning for Freedom and Other Essays and Addresses.* South Holland, Ill.: Libertarian Press, 1962.

——. *Socialism: An Economic and Sociological Analysis.* Translated by J. Kahane. New Haven: Yale University Press, 1951. This edition is translated from the second German edition (1932) of Mises's *Die Gemeinwirtschaft* (1922).

——. *The Theory of Money and Credit.* Irvington-on-Hudson, N.Y.: Foundation for Economic Education, 1971.

O'Driscoll, Gerald P., Jr. *Economics as a Coordination Problem: The Contributions of Friedrich A. Hayek.* Kansas City: Sheed Andrews & McMeel, 1977.

————, and Shenoy, Sudha R. "Inflation, Recession, and Stagflation." In *The Foundations of Modern Austrian Economics,* edited by Edwin G. Dolan, pp. 185–211. Kansas City: Sheed & Ward, 1976.

Palyi, Melchior. *The Inflation Primer.* Chicago: Regnery, 1972.

————. *The Twilight of Gold, 1914–1936: Myths and Realities.* Chicago: Regnery, 1972.

Raquet, Condy. *A Treatise on Currency and Banking.* New York: Kelley, 1967.

Rickenbacker, William F. *Death of the Dollar.* New York: Dell, 1970.

————. *Wooden Nickels, or the Decline and Fall of Silver Coins.* New Rochelle, N.Y.: Arlington House, 1966.

Ringer, Fritz. *The German Inflation of 1923.* New York: Oxford University Press, 1969.

Rist, Charles. *The Triumph of Gold.* Westport, Conn.: Greenwood, 1961.

————. *History of Monetary and Credit Theory.* New York: Kelley, 1966.

Robbins, Lionel. *The Great Depression.* Plainview, N.Y.: Books for Libraries, 1934.

Rothbard, Murray N. *America's Great Depression.* Kansas City: Sheed & Ward, 1975.

————. "Austrian Definitions of the Supply of Money." In *New Directions in Austrian Economics,* edited by Louis M. Spadaro, pp. 143–56. Kansas City: Sheed Andrews & McMeel, 1978.

————. "The Austrian Theory of Money." In *The Foundations of Modern Austrian Economics,* edited by Edwin G. Dolan, pp. 160–84. Kansas City: Sheed & Ward, 1976.

————. *The Case for a 100% Gold Dollar.* Alexandria, Va.: Libertarian Review Press, 1974.

————. *Man, Economy, and State: A Treatise on Economic Principles,* pp. 160–271, 661–759. Los Angeles: Nash, 1970.

————. *The Panic of 1819: Reaction and Policies.* New York: Columbia University Press, 1962.

———. *What Has Government Done to Our Money?* Novato, Calif.: Libertarian Publishers, 1978.

Rueff, Jacques. *The Age of Inflation*. Chicago: Regnery, 1964.

———. *Monetary Sin of the West*. New York: Macmillan, 1972.

Select Committee on the High Price of Gold, House of Commons. *The Paper Pound of 1797–1821*. New York: Kelley, 1969.

Sennholz, Hans, ed. *Gold Is Money*. Westport, Conn.: Greenwood, 1975.

Smith, Vera C. *The Rationale of Central Banking*. London: King, 1936.

Thornton, Henry. *An Inquiry into the Nature and Effects of the Paper Credit of Great Britain*. New York: Kelley, 1965.

Walker, Amasa. *The Science of Wealth*. Boston: Little, Brown, 1867.

Walker, Michael, ed. *The Illusion of Wage and Price Control: Essays on Inflation, Its Cause and Its Cures*. Vancouver, B.C.: Fraser Institute, 1976.

White, Andrew D. *Fiat Money Inflation in France*. Irvington-on-Hudson, N.Y.: Foundation for Economic Education, 1959.

Wicksell, G. Knut. *Interest and Prices: A Study of the Causes Regulating the Value of Money*. Clifton, N.J.: Kelley, 1965.

———. *Lectures on Political Economy*. Clifton, N.J.: Kelley, 1967–68.

Wiegand, G. Carl, ed. *The Menace of Inflation: Its Causes and Consequences*. Old Greenwich, Conn.: Devin-Adair, 1976.

Yeager, Leland B. "Essential Properties of a Medium of Exchange." *Kyklos,* 1968.

ABOUT THE AUTHOR

Friedrich Hayek, Dr Jur, Dr Sc Pol (University of Vienna), DSc (University of London), Visiting Professor at the University of Salzburg, Austria, 1970-74. Educated at the University of Vienna. Director, Austrian Institute for Business Cycle Research, 1927-31, and Lecturer in Economics at University of Vienna, 1929-31. Tooke Professor of Economic Science and Statistics, University of London, 1931-50. Professor of Social and Moral Science, University of Chicago, 1950-62. Professor of Economics, University of Freiburg, West Germany, 1962-68. He was awarded the Alfred Nobel Memorial Prize in Economic Science in 1974.

Professor Hayek is the author of *Choice in Currency: A Way to Stop Inflation; The Constitution of Liberty; The Counter-Revolution of Science: Studies on the Abuse of Reason; The Denationalisation of Money; Individualism and Economic Order; John Stuart Mill and Harriet Taylor; Law, Legislation and Liberty; Monetary Nationalism and International Stability; Monetary Theory and the Trade Cycle; New Studies in Philosophy, Politics, Economics and the History of Ideas; The Political Ideal of the Rule of Law; Prices and Production; Profits, Interest, Investments, and Other Essays on the Theory of Industrial Fluctuations; The Pure Theory of Capital; The Road to Serfdom; The Sensory Order; A Tiger by the Tail: The Keynesian Legacy of Inflation;* and many other works. He has edited or contributed to more than twenty volumes and is the author of more than 140 articles in scholarly journals around the world.

DATE DUE